Snorkelling with Nana

written by **Kelly Gaffney**

illustrated by Graham Smith

Gil's Nana and Grandpa lived
in a small house by the sea.
Grandpa loved to fish
and Nana loved to find pretty shells.
But what Nana loved to do
best of all was to snorkel.
Every time Gil came to visit,
he asked,
"Please, Nana, can you teach me
how to snorkel?"

And Nana would always say,
"When you're a bit older."

When Gil turned eight, he asked again.
"Please, Nana," said Gil,
"can you teach me how to snorkel?"

"Well," smiled Nana, "you're eight now...
and I know you're a good swimmer."

"Please!" begged Gil.

"Okay," laughed Nana. "Let's go!"

Nana, Grandpa and Gil walked
down to the beach.
When they came to Nana's favourite
snorkelling spot, Gil took out a snorkel
and some flippers from the bag.
While Nana helped Gil to get ready,
Grandpa got out his fishing rod.

When Nana and Gil were ready,
they walked carefully into the water.

Flip! Flop! Flip! Flop!

Gil and Nana laughed as they *flip-flopped* into the water.
Just then, a big wave rolled in and knocked Gil over.

Poor Gil! He got such a fright.

"I don't want to go snorkelling anymore," said Gil.

"I'm scared of the waves."

"Don't give up," smiled Nana.

"No!" said Gil. "I'm too scared."

"Well," said Nana sadly,
"you can play on the sand near Grandpa,
while I look at the fish."

Gil took off his flippers and snorkel,
and sat down.
He put on his hat and started
to build a sandcastle.
Gil looked up just as Nana popped
her head out of the water.
She waved to Gil.

"Nana looks as if she's having fun,"
said Grandpa.

Gil jumped up.

"Nana!" he shouted.

"I'm coming back in.

I want to see the beautiful fish!"

Nana swam back to the beach.

"Let's put on your flippers and snorkel,"
she said.

Gil took Nana's hand as they walked
back into the sea.

"Look!" shouted Gil.

"Here comes a big wave!"

But he didn't go back to Grandpa.

He held onto Nana's hand

as the big wave pushed against them.

"Well done," smiled Nana.

"Let's swim towards the little rocks."

"This is fun, Nana!" said Gil,
as his head popped up beside her.
"I can see lots of beautiful fish."

Gil and Nana snorkelled for a long time.
They saw lots of colourful fish.

At last, they went back to the beach.
"Thank you for teaching me how
to snorkel," said Gil.
"I was scared at first,
but I'm glad I tried again."

"I'm glad you tried again, too,"
smiled Nana.
"Snorkelling is my favourite thing to do.
Now you can always come with me!"